Henry VIII's Interesting Bits

Written and drawn
by Fay Gregory

Barker Books

Barker Books, "White House", The Warren, Ashtead, Surrey, England.

Henry VIII's Interesting Bits

First Published 1993
Reprinted 1994, 1995 and 1996

ISBN 0 9521603 0 7

Printed in Great Britain by Abbey Green Printers, Chertsey, Surrey.

Anne Boleyn,
Henry's second wife.

Contents

Introduction

Everyone's heard of King Henry VIII. He was the fat one who married six times. But did you know that he banned football and that one of his wives had 3 breasts? Did you know that he only grew a beard because the French king had one? Or that his ghost is said to haunt Windsor Castle?

Whether you use it as a school or home study aid, or just read it for fun, this book will tell you all you need to know about this fascinating character. The timeline helps to set everything in it's correct time and with over seventy illustrations it's an easy way to learn new facts or brush up on old ones.

The Tudor Rose.

Timeline

1491	Birth of Henry.
1509	Henry VII dies and Henry VIII becomes king.
	Henry marries Catherine of Aragon.
1512	Wolsey rises to power.
1513	Henry invades France and wins the Battle of the Spurs.
	The Scots are defeated at the Battle of Flodden.
1520	The Field of the Cloth of Gold.
1522	At war with France again.
1525	Henry makes peace with France.
1527	Divorce proceedings are started against Catherine.
1530	Cardinal Wolsey dies.
1531	Henry declares himself head of the Church of England.
1533	Henry marries Anne Boleyn.
1535	Bishop Fisher and Thomas More are executed.
	The Pope excommunicates Henry.
1536	Catherine of Aragon dies aged 50.
	Anne Boleyn is executed aged 35.
	Henry marries Jane Seymour.
1537	Edward VI is born, and Jane Seymour dies aged 28.
1540	Henry marries and divorces Anne of Cleves.
1542	Scotland is defeated at Solway Moss.
	Catherine Howard is executed aged 21.
1543	Henry marries Catherine Parr.
1544	Edinburgh is raided and Boulogne captured.
1545	The Mary-Rose sinks.
1546	Henry makes peace with France again.
1547	Henry dies.
1548	Catherine Parr dies aged 36.
1553	Edward VI dies.
1557	Anne of Cleves dies aged 41.

Catherine of Aragon's Interesting Bits

The most well known fact about Henry is that he was married 6 times, partly because he wanted a son to inherit the throne. A number of wives would have fared much better if they had been able to supply a baby boy.

Catherine of Aragon had boys but they were either stillborn or died young, which was quite common in those days. She eventually bore Henry 6 children (Mary Tudor was one of them) only to be divorced so he could marry Anne Boleyn. The strange thing was that everybody knew Henry already had a son after an affair with a Mistress Bessie Blount. The boy was named Henry Fitzroy, Duke of Richmond, and died at the age of 17.

Catherine was a Spanish princess, the daughter of Isabella and Ferdinand (who were themselves famous for their dealings with Columbus), and had already been married to Henry's brother (see Interesting Religious Bits). She was 6 years older than Henry and was short, even by 16th. century standards.

Women in Spanish dress were said to resemble devils.

Apparently she liked monkeys and was a keen gardener.

Catherine was a strong character who managed to stay with Henry for 22 years but when he divorced her she never got over it. He banished her and her staff of 200 to relative poverty near Peterborough where she continued to write to him until she died. He never returned her letters.

Catherine sewed all of Henry's shirts herself.

At her death it was rumoured that Henry had poisoned her, but the surgeons found a lump on her heart which led everyone to believe that she died of a broken heart. She probably died of cancer.

Catherine was a keen gardener.

Henry eventually decided he would prefer to be interred with Jane Seymour rather than Catherine, in a tomb which Wolsey was intending to use, so Catherine was buried in Peterborough Cathedral. Henry and Jane are in St. George's Chapel, Windsor Castle, but the tomb is in St. Paul's Cathedral with Lord Nelson inside!

Interesting Religious Bits

When Henry VIII came to the throne, England was a Catholic country, and, as the head of the church, the Pope was treated with great respect and regarded as God's right hand man.

Henry was very religious. He read, wrote and talked a lot about his religion, and the Pope was pleased to have such a keen Catholic on the English throne.

Look at a coin and find the letters F.D.

They stand for 'Defender of the Faith', a title given to Henry by the Pope as a reward for being such a good Catholic.

As you know, Catherine of Aragon had been married before.....to Henry's big brother, Arthur. Many people had said that it would be wrong for Henry to marry his dead brother's wife but when the Pope was asked he said it would be O.K.

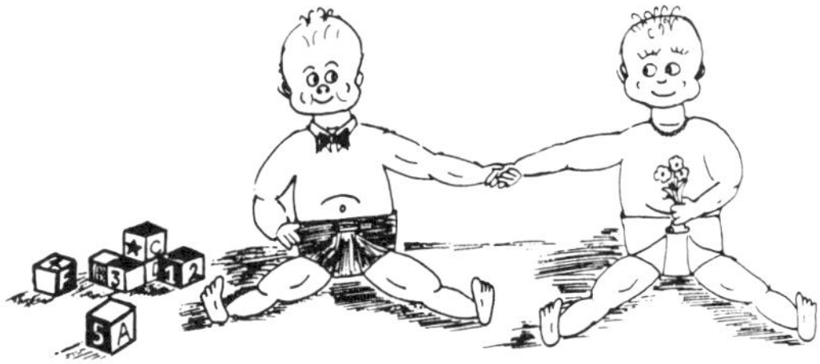

Catherine and Arthur married very young. When Arthur died he was only 15, and Catherine was a widow at 16 years old.

Things began to go wrong when Henry decided that if Catherine couldn't provide him with a son, he would find someone else who could! He asked the Pope to allow a divorce because he should never have married his dead brother's wife in the first place! The Pope refused, mostly because Catherine's nephew was threatening to attack him if he didn't, and Henry decided to take matters into his own hands.

Henry was responsible for the first English Bible.

Pity so many couldn't read.

Henry made himself head of the Church of England and gave himself a divorce. The fact that he secretly married the pregnant Anne Boleyn before he divorced Catherine didn't seem to matter!

This one doesn't work.
I'd like a new one, please.

Catherine was pregnant 6 times, but only one child survived...... and it was a girl.

When Henry ran out of money, he dissolved (closed) the monasteries and took their wealth for himself.

A monastery being dissolved.

The Pope wasn't impressed, and as far as he was concerned, things got worse and worse. Henry dissolved all the monasteries to raise funds and was extremely harsh with anyone who stood in the way.

A large number of Catholics including monks, nuns, and abbots were brutally put to death by being burned at the stake or hanged, drawn and quartered. Some were chained to immovably heavy weights and left to starve.

Abbots who refused to hand over their monasteries were burned at the stake.

Surprisingly, although the public were shocked at the way their king had disobeyed the Pope, they were quite pleased about the monasteries closing. They felt that many monks had become fat, lazy and greedy, and weren't doing what they were supposed to - looking after travellers, or caring for the poor and ill.

The duties of a monk had changed over the years.

Even some of the monks were pleased. Often their fathers had forced them into the church at an early age, and they were delighted to leave the quiet and dull monasteries.

Finally the Pope could take no more and Henry was excommunicated from the Catholic church. This meant Henry had no chance of going to heaven after his death, but he obviously didn't mind.

Henry was made to feel unwelcome in Rome.

Cardinal Wolsey's Interesting Bits

Wolsey was the son of a butcher.

Thomas Wolsey was born the son of a butcher but went to school and earned an Oxford degree at the age of fifteen. A succession of church posts led to a chaplaincy at the court of Henry VII, and when King Henry VIII showed that he was more interested in hunting than running the country, Wolsey leapt at the chance to take charge.

Thomas Wolsey

Gradually he was awarded bishoprics and then made a cardinal, but his true ambition was to become Pope. Despite his vows of celibacy and his religious role, he had a son and hardly ever visited any of his religious seats.

He was a workaholic, greedy for riches and magnificence, and had a terrible temper, but he was an intelligent man and, through clever negotiations, was responsible for England's rise to a powerful European state.

Wolsey had a terrible temper. He would go to bed in case he said anything he might later regret.

Wolsey loved the good life. He ran a household of 800, built himself beautiful palaces (Hampton Court and York Place, later known as Whitehall), and held such lavish banquets that many began to wonder exactly who was the king.

When money was tight, Wolsey sent his jester as a gift.

The fall from power began when Wolsey failed to persuade the Pope to allow Henry and Catherine of Aragon to divorce, and Anne Boleyn didn't help by telling Henry that Wolsey was purposely obstructing their marriage.

Henry stripped Wolsey of all his palaces and riches, and on 29th November 1530, on his way to a trial which would almost certainly have resulted in execution, Wolsey died in Leicester.

Anne Boleyn's Interesting Bits

Anne Boleyn was a colourful character and is historically important as she was the mother of Elizabeth I. Henry thought her a beautiful woman, but other sources were not as complimentary, one referring to her as a "goggle eyed whore".

Elizabeth 1 was Anne's daughter.

Anne had very long black hair, three breasts and the shadow of a sixth finger on one hand! She was pregnant when she married Henry, and was the second wife to bear him a stillborn son. She was hated by the population who thought she was calculating and scheming, and nicknamed her the Black Crow.

Anne Boleyn's hair was so long, she could sit upon it in her litter.

A litter was a chair carried by a man at each end.

In common with her husband, Anne enjoyed music, books and hunting but disliked the garden peacocks and pelicans so much that they had to be caged.

Anne Boleyn's badge shows a crowned falcon.

At her coronation, the crowds shouted "Ha Ha" in reference to their entwined initials on the draperies. 50 barges, all holding minstrels, took part in the ceremony and so much artillery was fired that the glass fell out of all the local windows.

After only three years of marriage, her nagging, temper-tantrums and flirting, aswell as the fact that she had still not produced a son, displeased Henry enough to set him looking for a replacement. Charged with treason, Anne was imprisoned in the Tower. After some months sharing a cell with a Mrs. Coffin(!), she was executed.

Anne Boleyn hated the garden peacocks and pelicans so much that they had to be caged.

Anne has been busy since her death, appearing in a number of different places (see Interesting Ghostly Bits).

Interesting Sporty Bits

Henry was a great sportsman and took part in a wide variety of activities, so much so that the running of the country was left almost entirely to Cardinal Wolsey.

He was an energetic tennis player and had a court built at Hampton Court, where "real tennis" is still played. He played hard and a spectator noticed that the king's skin glowed through his white tennis shirt!

Game, set and match!

There is a rumour that he was playing tennis when Anne Boleyn was executed, but another story says he was out hunting, waiting on high ground for the gunfire that would signal Anne's execution.

When Henry played tennis a full set of balls numbered 9 dozen (that's 108!).

Henry spent a lot of time hunting deer, foxes and wild boar, and he could wear out up to 10 horses before he'd finished. He seemed to take everything to extremes, and when jousting, he once used 286 spears in one tournament.

On one occasion, Henry was jousting with his brother-in-law and forgot to lower the visor of his helmet. The crowd shouted warnings, but Henry thought they were just calling out words of encouragement and carried on. His opponent's lance shattered into tiny splinters which flew into Henry's helmet, but luckily the king escaped unhurt.

Henry's love of jousting often ended in accidents.

He used to attend tournaments in disguise and, on winning, would throw off his cover and "surprise" the crowd. However, the crowd, and the losing opponents were usually simply playing the game as, even in disguise, Henry's size gave him away.

NO FOOTBALL

Other sporting interests included hawking, archery and javelin throwing, and he also liked to watch wrestling, which was a popular spectator sport at fairs and on holidays. Football, however was the cause of much fighting and rioting and so Henry banned it altogether.

Interesting Execution Bits 1

Hangings often included being cut open whilst still alive, and because so many crimes were punishable by death, the gallows were often very crowded.

Commoners were hanged but privileged noblemen were allowed the faster and less painful beheading.

I wish he'd hurry up, I hate hanging around.

Henry was responsible for the deaths of more than one thousand people including Anne Boleyn, her brother and "lovers", Catherine Howard and her lovers; the advisers Thomas More and Cromwell, and Bishop John Fisher. Wolsey would probably have been executed had he not died of natural causes, and Catherine Parr also had a close shave (see her page). The French ambassador said "there was no head so fine that he (Henry) would not make it fly".

Henry employed a French swordsman to execute Anne Boleyn so she wouldn't have to suffer the axe.

When the executioner showed her head to the crowd, her eyes and lips were still moving!

Beheaded heads were impaled on spears on London Bridge where they went black in the sun.

When Henry split the English church from Rome, many people disagreed with his actions. Thomas More was one man who refused to recognise Henry as the head of the church, and so he, like dozens of others, was executed on a charge of treason (see Interesting Religious Bits).

Don't burn in the sun, use new 'TUDOR TAN'.

The goriest of the beheadings must be that of Margaret Pole, the 70 year old Countess of Salisbury. She refused to place her head on the block like a traitor, and so the executioner took a swing where she stood. However, she kept moving away, and the axeman had to follow her, cutting into her shoulders and neck many times before she finally died (see ghosts page).

Jane Seymour's Interesting Bits

Jane Seymour was an intelligent woman who tried not to become involved wih Henry. She returned letters unopened, aswell as gifts and wouldn't talk to him unless they were in company.

Jane Seymour was a keen gardener.
Friends often received cucumbers as presents.

Jane was working as one of Anne Boleyn's maids when Henry first noticed her. They got engaged the very next day after Anne Boleyn's execution!

Jane was a real angel!

She enjoyed gardening and other gentle pursuits, and was a sweet and virtuous woman of whom no-one spoke badly. It was reported that she was "no great beauty", but that she was famous for her fashionably pure white skin.

Jane Seymour's badge shows a phoenix rising from a castle.

When Jane was heavily pregnant, she followed tradition and was confined to bed. Henry was absent at the birth, having gone to the country to avoid an outbreak of plague.

With the aid of Tudor surgery, Jane gave birth to a son, Edward, but probably as a result of dirty instruments, she contracted puerperal fever and died 12 days later.

Jane would pluck her hairline to be fashionable.

The famous picture which shows Henry, Jane Seymour and their son Edward was never possible in real life as Jane died when Edward was only days old.

Henry was truly heart-broken and arranged for her to be buried in St. George's Chapel, Windsor, where he was to be buried himself.

Interesting Healthy Bits

In his youth, Henry was certainly a handsome man. At over six feet, he was unusually tall and had a slim and athletic figure. He liked physical activity (see Interesting Sporty Bits) and his many outdoor pursuits no doubt helped him to enjoy good health. However, good health did not prevent him from being a terrible hypochondriac; he was so terrified of sickness and plague that he would flee to the country at the slightest hint of an outbreak.

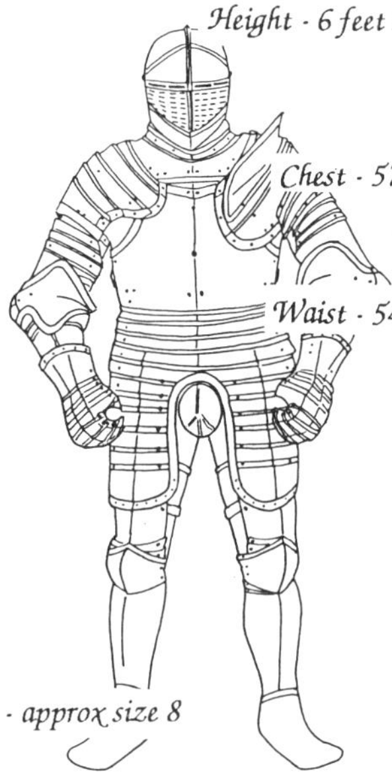

Henry's armour shows just how big he was.

Despite his best efforts, Henry was unable to prevent the decline which accompanied the approach of middle age. He suffered from bouts of fever, smallpox, malaria and was prone to severe migraine headaches. His legs became ulcerated and swollen, effectively putting a stop to his healthy outdoor life which in turn caused him to put on weight.

Henry got so fat he had to be carried around in a litter.

He was reluctant to give up his riding, however, and was even willing to be winched onto his horse!

At home, Henry was eventually so totally immobile that he had to be carried everywhere in a litter and moved around the house with pulleys and more winches.

After a long illness, he died obese, in pain and, some say, with the balance of his mind disturbed.

Henry did <u>not</u> explode.

It took the strength of 16 soldiers to move Henry's coffin, and there have been rumours that his corpse exploded owing to a build-up of rotting gases. There is no truth in this, however, as his coffin lies, almost perfect, in the crypt of St. George's chapel, Windsor.

Interesting Hobby Bits

Whatever Henry was, he certainly wasn't boring. Apart from his numerous sporting activities (see Interesting Sporty Bits) he also enjoyed more intellectual pursuits.

He owned 78 recorders.

Henry had recorders coming out of his ears.

He was a talented musician and played a variety of instruments including the virginal (an early harpsichord), lute (like a guitar), harp, organ, flute and recorder. He also composed music for the Chapel choir in Hampton Court and took a great interest in singing and writing part-songs and masses.

He might have written "Greensleeves" for Anne Boleyn, but he sometimes changed the odd note of other mens' tunes and then called them his own, so it's difficult to know whether he really wrote it or not.

Henry was an accomplished player of the lyre.

As well as playing instruments and singing, Henry loved dancing and was always keen to take to the floor.

He enjoyed astronomy and used to go onto the roof of Hampton Court to view the night skies.

Gambling on whether a man could eat a whole buck deer, or whether a greyhound could kill a cow was one way to fill a few hours, and unlikely as it might seem, he could spend just as many hours discussing controversial religious topics.

Henry was a keen gambler.

Henry was good at designing castles.

Guns and weaponry were another interest. He established an armoury at Greenwich and supported research into new cast-iron guns, taking a personal interest in any progress. At Portsmouth one of his officers remarked that the king would ask for cannon to be fired again and again, noting changes in trajectory and range. Still on the subject of defence, Henry loved geometry and often designed castles and machines.

He was a great linguist and could speak French, Spanish, Greek and Latin. Unfortunately, he didn't speak German and so was unable to converse with wife number 4, Anne of Cleves.

One of Henry's least favourite occupations was writing. He hated it and rarely wrote anything himself, leaving this "somewhat tedious and painful" task to his advisors.

Thomas More's Interesting Bits

Thomas More was a great scholar.

Thomas More was a trained lawyer and one of the greatest scholars of his time. A man of European reputation, he could be witty and serious, gentle and strong, and was called "a man for all seasons". However, his support for the Catholic church prevented him from accepting Henry as the spiritual head of the new Church of England, and he went to the block for his beliefs.

At first, Henry's affection and respect allowed him to ignore More's disapproval, but More knew this wouldn't last. When Henry appointed him chancellor, More was reluctant to take up the post, and soon after he resigned on the grounds of poor health. In fact it was because his conscience wouldn't let him fully support his king.

Thomas More

When More persistently refused to give his support, he was sent to the Tower where he lived for over a year. Like all prisoners, he paid for his keep and for some time he was quite comfortable. Eventually, conditions were made harsher and his books and writing materials were confiscated, so he wrote to his daughter using a piece of coal.

When victims were ready they would stretch their arms out as a signal to the executioner.

More moved his beard from the block as he said that had never committed treason.

On 1st July 1536, More was led to the scaffold. His daughter, Margaret, rushed sobbing to him and had to be pulled away by the guards in a scene which touched all the onlookers.

Simmer gently for 40 minutes.

Before he was beheaded, he moved his beard aside saying, "that has never committed any treason", and later, as was usual with traitors, his head was parboiled and displayed on London Bridge.

More was not as guiltless as he sometimes appears and was responsible for the persecution and burning of many heretics.

Anne of Cleves' Interesting Bits

Henry agreed to marry Anne of Cleves on the strength of a picture which he later felt had been rather too flattering.

It wasn't a good first meeting. Henry arrived unexpectedly and Anne, not recognising him, continued to look out of the window at the bull-baiting. Henry was none too pleased and left the room, returning in more obviously royal clothes so they could start again.

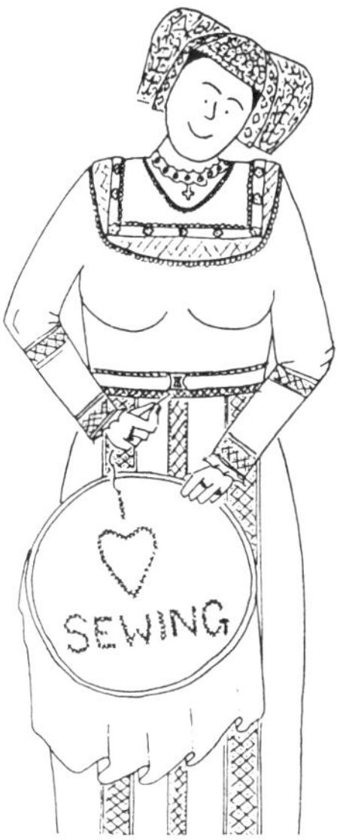

Anne of Cleves enjoyed tapestry.

Anne wasn't a good match for Henry. She wasn't well educated, neither played an instrument, nor danced nor sang, and when she first came to England she didn't even speak English. She wasn't keen on outdoor activities either and a courtier said that "she occupieth her time mostly with a needle".

Anne of Cleves' badge.

Flippin' cheek!

He was furious when he first set eyes on her, calling her a "Flanders Mare", and refusing to go through with the wedding. Unfortunately, no-one could find a reason as to why he and Anne should not marry so it went ahead at 8a.m. on 6th. January 1540.

The marriage was never consummated, (she didn't know the facts of life even after marrying the king!) , and lasted a mere 6 months until Henry divorced her because she had been engaged before. It's said that when the news of the divorce arrived, she fainted because she had been expecting an execution order.

When Henry agreed to marry Anne, he'd never seen her before.

After their divorce, Anne was made Henry's adopted sister and she passed her years in a happy, homely existence, running her estates and taking an active interest in Henry's children, Elizabeth, Mary and Edward.

She began to enjoy living in England and became popular with her servants and the public who thought her "gracious and humane". She died at the age of 42 after a long illness, probably cancer.

Interesting Torture Bits

Life in Tudor times was hard, and so, it seems, were the people. Without a police force, they took the law into their own hands and treated criminals severely to set an example to others. Common punishments for minor crimes included branding, whipping, and being put into the stocks or pillory; more serious penalties resulted in hands, ears, and noses being cut off; and for crimes such as treason and murder, most criminals were executed by hanging, burning or boiling.

The Pillory

But before fingerprinting and forensics were around, it wasn't easy to prove someone's guilt, so instruments of torture were used to extract confessions.

The Stocks

Iron Collar

The most commonly used tortures in Henry's time were the rack and the Scavenger's Daughter. This was an iron frame which could crush a man's body until the blood ran from his nostrils and fingertips. The rack pulled the body in opposite directions, tearing muscles and dislocating joints until the victim confessed or passed out. Under such treatment, many victims were prepared to admit anything, but a few, like Anne Askew, still refused to speak. She was racked for her religious beliefs and, being unable to walk afterwards, was tied into a chair and carried to the stake to be burnt.

I do love a good stretch in the morning.

Edmund Campion was martyred after Henry's reign, but his condition graphically illustrates the effects of the rack; he was brought to the Tower with his elbows tied behind him and his hands tied in front, and with his legs tied together under the horse's belly.

Many prisoners entered the Tower through Traitors' Gate.

Between rackings in the Tower dungeons, prisoners were sometimes kept in "Little Ease", a cell which was so small it was impossible to lie or even sit down. A stay of four days was quite common.

Other instruments of torture included brakes which broke a prisoner's teeth; thumbscrews and pilliwinks which crushed the fingers; and iron collars and boots, the purpose of which has been forgotten. Alternatively, prisoners could be suspended by the wrists, have the soles of their feet burnt, or be subjected to a maddening constant drip of water on the forehead.

Most torture took place in the Tower of London.

Anne Boleyn's minstrel had a knotted rope twisted around his head with a cudgel until he admitted to the charges against him.

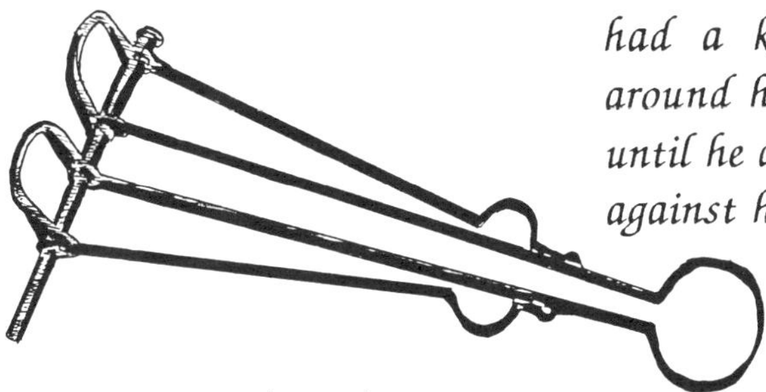

Scavenger's Daughter

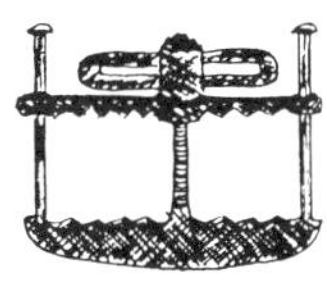

Thumbscrews

Pressing to death meant tying the victim down and placing heavy weights on his body until his bones broke. Added to this, food and water was given on alternate days; Monday, food; Tuesday, water and so on. This punishment was developed as it was considered more humane than simply starving the prisoner to death.

Interesting Execution Bits 2

Bishop John Fisher was kept in the Tower for a year before he was sent to the block, by which time he was so old and feeble that he had to rest three times between his cell and the scaffold. It was Fisher's cook who poisoned beggars and was boiled to death in oil.

Bishop Fisher's cook was executed by being boiled slowly in oil.

I see a tall handsome stranger.....with an axe.

A nun from Canterbury, Elizabeth Barton, (also known as the "Holy Maid of Kent"), told Henry that if he married Anne Boleyn, he would die a villain's death and cease being king within a month. Henry married Anne anyway, and the nun was hanged with 5 companions.

Five more were dragged to Tyburn to be hanged, drawn and quartered, and one arm was hung over the monastery door to warn others not to disagree with the king.

For causing an uprising, one tax-man was hanged and another was sewn into a cow skin and fed to hungry dogs.

The axe and execution block.

Burning at the stake was a long and agonising way to die, so friends would place bags of gun-powder in the wood pile to speed the victim's death.

Business has never been so good.

Interesting Ghostly Bits

Whether you believe in ghosts or not, many people claim to have seen or heard things which can only be described as supernatural.

Ghosts and spooky goings-on are often thought to be caused by a terrible experience or tragedy which prevents peaceful rest after death. If this is so, it would be surprising if there were no ghosts associated with Henry VIII. as he was a cruel and barbaric man who caused suffering to hundreds of families. It's said that over a thousand people were tortured or executed on Henry's orders.

There are lots of ghosts in Hampton Court.

Hampton Court is the place to go to see Anne Boleyn gliding through corridors, Edward VI's nurse spinning, or Jane Seymour walking with a lighted candle. It's the place where Catherine Howard's white ghost glides screaming through the Long Gallery, a memory of when she tried to persuade Henry to cancel the execution order. You have to be quick, 'though, because she disappears as soon as she is seen.

Anne Boleyn has appeared headless in two places within the Tower. She has been seen by sentries, and some of them have even charged at her and seen their bayonets go straight through to the wall behind! She has also appeared headless at her birth place, Blickling Hall in Norfolk, travelling in a coach drawn by horses, also headless.

Jane Seymour haunts Hampton Court.

But she was here just now!

Henry has not been seen, but a lame man has been heard dragging his feet along a walk in Windsor Castle. The very walk that Henry took when his legs became too painful for riding.

Cardinal Wolsey was spotted in his famous red outfit, at a son et lumiere show at Hampton Court.

Cardinal Wolsey.

The best place for ghosts is the Tower of London. One of the most spine-chilling is that of Margaret Pole (see Interesting Execution Bits) whose ghost reportedly runs screaming from the axeman on the anniversary of her death.

During works in the Tower of London Chapel, bodies were found everywhere including under the floor and in the walls. Some were whole, but many had been separated from their heads and this might explain the large number of unidentified headless ghosts which have been sighted.

It is worth mentioning that even recently a number of Hampton Court workers have felt the need to find work elsewhere after seeing ghosts.

Catherine Howard's Interesting Bits

A cousin of Anne Boleyn, Catherine Howard was brought up by an aged relative and made her friends amongst the servants. They enjoyed encouraging her teenage crushes and, as a result, she had associated with a number of men before she caught Henry's eye whilst working as a maid at court.

The King's wife was expected to be pure and unsullied, so in order to become and remain queen, Catherine had to ensure that Henry would not discover her guilty past. This became more and more difficult as the servants she had earlier befriended returned to blackmail her.

Catherine Howard was really tiny!

It is almost impossible to know what Catherine looked like. Reports say that she was reasonably attractive and that she dressed in a French style, but there are no pictures to bear this out.

Catherine found her step-daughter difficult to get on with, and as Catherine was 5 years younger than Mary, it was certainly a strange situation. Anne of Cleves was a great friend, however, and Catherine and Anne used to dance together regularly.

They married on the same day that Cromwell, Henry's close advisor, was beheaded, and Henry was delighted with his new wife. She was young (30 years younger than Henry), attractive, full of life, and a great comfort to an old and sick man. At first he showered her with gifts and it was noted that he couldn't keep his hands off her, even in public. He also asked that she did not see him when he was ill.

Henry showered Catherine with gifts.

Catherine Howard's badge.

Very quickly rumours began to spread about her flirting and although Henry initially refused to believe them, the evidence grew too great to be ignored and he wept openly when her infidelity was proven.

After less than 18 months of marriage, she was sentenced to death and sent to the Tower where she practised with the block in her cell. She was executed as a traitor at the age of 21. (See Interesting Ghostly Bits).

Interesting Defensive Bits

Although Henry is famous as the only English monarch to marry six times, and perhaps as one of the most violent kings, he deserves to be remembered in a more positive way as a king who made England strong.

'This isn't quite what I had in mind'.

After years of peace under his father's rule, Henry reopened hostilities firstly with the French and later with the Holy Roman Empire. He sent fighting dogs with spiked collars to the Spanish so that they could attack the French too, and then, expecting attack, he set about defending his own country by establishing a more powerful navy.

Henry sent trained fighting dogs to Spain

He increased the number of ships and improved their fire power by inventing portholes.
This meant extra guns could be placed on lower decks, and with gunports at the bow and stern the ship could now fire in every direction.

Henry spent a lot of time developing the navy.

He built it up from 7 ships to 53.

The ill-fated Mary Rose was one of Henry's most powerful ships.

The Coast

Henry also spent time and money ensuring that the land, particularly ports and landing sites, was well defended. No less than twenty new fortifications appeared along the south coast and many existing older forts were strengthened and improved. Altogether Henry's line of defence stretched from Cornwall to Kent.

Finding enough building stone for all this might have been a problem, but Henry simply knocked down the monasteries and recycled the stone; in some castle walls you can still see stones with religious carvings, revealing their earlier function.

Mary Rose's Interesting Bits

The Mary Rose was Henry's favourite ship.

When the French attacked England in 1545, Mary-Rose was put into action. In full view of Henry VIII, Catherine Parr and hundreds of sailors' families, she turned out of Portsmouth harbour to defend her country.

The numbers of guns and extra soldiers on deck possibly made the ship top-heavy, and when she turned too quickly, the ship began to keel over. Water flooded in through the gunports on the lower decks and she sank quickly.

Her sister ship was the Peter Pomegranate!

Mary Rose

Peter Pomegranate!

Nets which had been hung down the sides of the hull to prevent the enemy from boarding through the gun ports, now prevented the crew from escaping.

Few sailors learnt to swim so even those who managed to leave the ship drowned and as a result, nearly all 700 hands were lost.

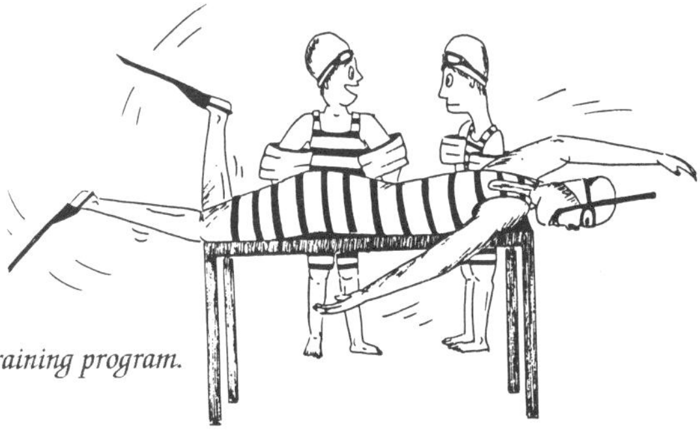

It's part of the new training program.

For some unknown reason, the French did not follow up their attack, but turned and fled.

Over 400 years later, Mary-Rose was gently raised to the surface again. The remains of the ship and hundreds of artefacts showing how sailors lived on board ship can be seen in Portsmouth.

Amongst the finds were clothes, wooden bowls and tankards, bows and arrows, writing equipment, medicines, musical instruments, a backgammon set and dice.

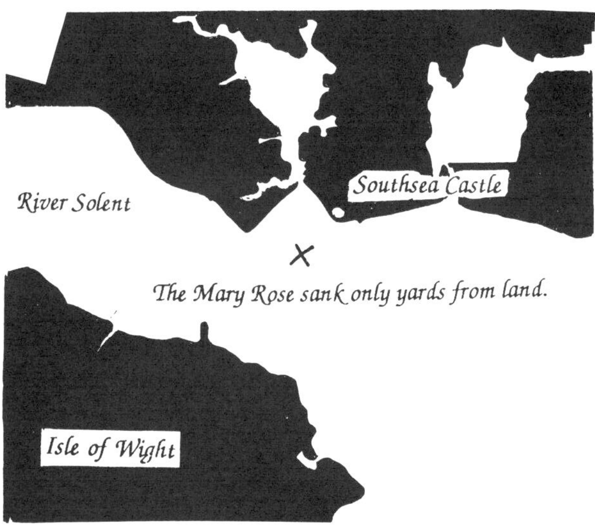

The Mary Rose sank only yards from land.

When The Mary Rose was raised, they discovered a large quantity of black pepper. This was found in the surgeon's cabin and had been used to combat flatulence.

Catherine Parr's Interesting Bits

Although many thought that Henry would, and should, remarry Anne of Cleves, Catherine Parr was Henry's sixth wife, and Henry was her third husband. She had been married to two other men who had both died, each leaving her his wealth. Consequently, from fairly poor beginnings, she had become an exceedingly rich woman.

It only needs the hem turning up, madam.

Catherine dressed well, inheriting her predecessor, Catherine Howard's clothes, as the richly embroidered gowns were highly expensive to produce, and she owned lots of shoes: she ordered 47 pairs in just one year!

Catherine Parr's badge shows a girl rising from a Tudor rose.

She won't be long, she's just choosing some shoes.

Catherine was a lively and active woman. She loved learning and was intelligent, and had a pleasant character. She was tall and elegant, with auburn hair, but she was never described as a beauty. Even Anne of Cleves, who was not renowned for her own good looks, thought Catherine was less attractive than she was.

Where have you put my glasses?!!!

Henry's health was deteriorating fast. His legs were more and more painful, his failing eyesight had forced him to use reading glasses, and despite his worsening tempers, Catherine was always there to care for him. Many courtiers disapproved of Catherine's religious beliefs (they were different to Henry's) and persuaded Henry, whose mental health was unstable, to sign a warrant for her arrest. The document fell into Catherine's hands and she managed to talk him out of it.

Apart from her pet greyhounds and parrots, she shared Henry's love of music, having her own consort of viols.

Catherine had lots and lots of shoes!

When he died, Catherine watched as he was laid to rest with Jane Seymour.

Soon after, she married another Seymour, her former sweetheart, and had a child. Sadly, Catherine died only days later. Her husband (who once made inappropriate advances towards Princess Elizabeth) was later beheaded for treason.

Interesting Battle Bits

Henry's reign was not a particularly peaceful one, with fighting between England and France, Spain and Scotland.

Catherine of Aragon's father persuaded Henry to invade France with him, but the soldiers refused to fight and came home because their beer had gone sour!

Henry appointed Wolsey to sort out the army, which he did brilliantly, and the next invasion was known as the "Battle of the Spurs" as all the English saw were the retreating spurs of the French cavalry. The French responded by getting Scotland to invade England, but at the Battle of Flodden the Scots were heavily defeated and their king, James IV, was killed.

The King of France looked very similar to Henry.

Francois I

Peace with France was reached when Henry turned against the Spanish and met his old rival Francois I at the famous Field of the Cloth of Gold. Henry resented Francois who was younger, just as good looking and likely to take Henry's place as the new star of the European monarchy. So when Francois grew a beard, so did Henry and there were long discussions about whose legs were the most shapely!

The Field of the Cloth of Gold was in a part of France which then belonged to England, and was so called because everyone spent a fortune trying to impress the other side.

Henry arriving at the Field of the Cloth of Gold....

It was said that the nobles wore their estates on their backs, and many were financially ruined by the event.

To show their friendship, Henry and Francois rode hand in hand for a mile, but peace was short-lived and war broke out only two years later with Henry turning back to the Spanish.

Spain became very powerful and defeated Francois I and so England, for the right price, joined the French again!

.....and meeting Francois I.

Things never really calmed down between Scotland and England and as well as raids on Edinburgh, acts of piracy continued on the North Sea for many years.

Other Interesting Bits

A selection of interesting bits that wouldn't fit anywhere else!

As a young man, Henry used to throw ornaments off his clothes to the crowds.

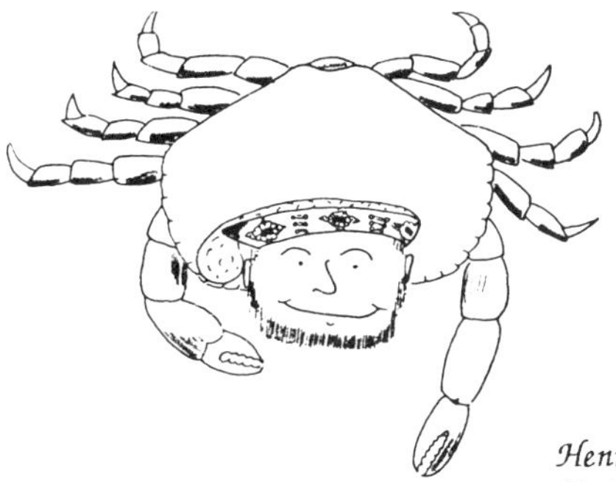

Henry's birthday was 28th June so his birthsign was cancer.

When Henry was 10 years old, his brother, Arthur, married Catherine of Aragon. Henry marked the occasion by dancing in his underwear.

This weapon, which incorporates a spear, axe and even a pistol, is in the Tower of London. It was known as a 'Holy Water Sprinkler', or 'Henry VIII's Walking Stick'.

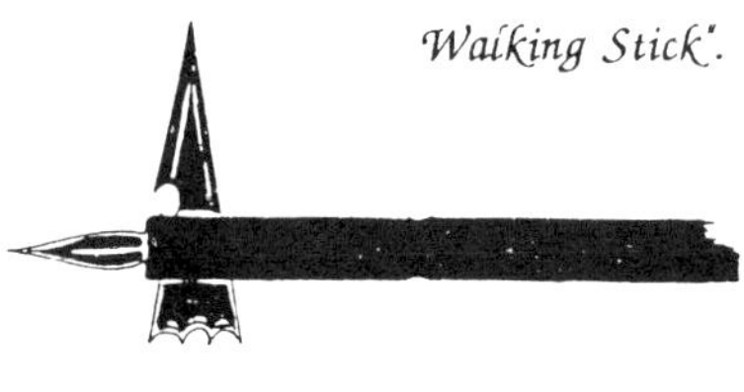

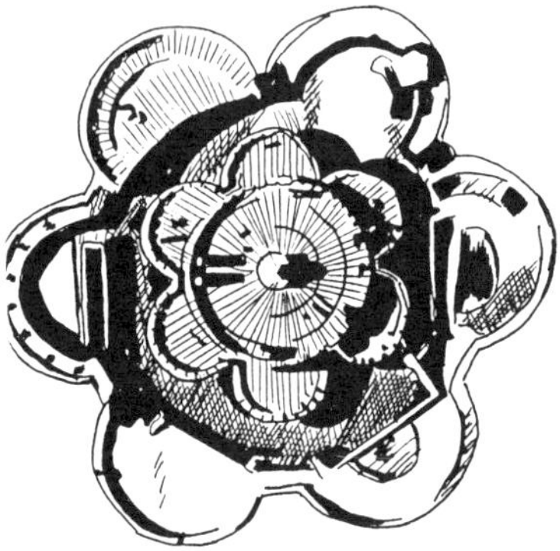

Henry's castles were a particular design. They had low towers as this was thought to reduce the enemy's target and they were round to deflect enemy shots. Deal is a good example of this design.

Obesity altered Henry's features in old age.

This famous rhyme helps to remember what happened to Henry's wives.

Divorced	*Catherine of Aragon*
Beheaded	*Anne Boleyn*
Died	*Jane Seymour*
Divorced	*Anne of Cleves*
Beheaded	*Catherine Howard*
Survived	*Catherine Parr*

Index

Mary Tudor, Henry's daughter

Henry's Family

Henry VIII

I

I	I	I	I	I	I
(1)	(2)	(3)	(4)	(5)	(6)
Catherine of Aragon (d.1536)	Anne Boleyn (d.1536)	Jane Seymour (d.1537)	Anne of Cleves (d.1557)	Catherine Howard (d.1542)	Catherine Parr (d.1548)
I	I	I			
Mary 1 (r.1553-58)	Elizabeth 1 (r.1558-1603)	Edward VI (r.1547-53)			